WHAT·DO·WE·KNOW

ABOUT
JUDAISM·?

DOREEN FINE

PETER BEDRICK BOOKS

NEW YORK

Published by
Peter Bedrick Books
2112 Broadway
New York, NY 10023

© ~~MD~~ Macdonald Young Books Ltd 1995

Published by agreement with Macdonald Young Books Ltd, England

Designer and illustrator: Celia Hart
Commissioning editor: Debbie Fox
Editors: Caroline Arthur, Lesley Taylor
Picture research: Jane Taylor
Consultant: Laurie Rosenberg, Executive Director of Education, Board of Deputies of British Jews

Photograph acknowledgements: Front and back cover: Stewart Weir; Andes Press Agency, pp8, 41(b) (Carlos Reyes-Manzo); Architectural Association, p21(b) (John Ross); MS Kennicott 1 Folio 305^R, Bodleian Library Oxford; Anat Rotem-Braun, Jerusalem, pp15(l), 29(t), 31(c); Werner Braun, Jerusalem, p33(b); Bridgeman Art Library, pp13(t) Giraudon/ "Jacob's Dream" by Ludovico Cardi da Cigoli (1559–1613), Musée des Beaux-Arts, Nancy, 14 "Moses and the Tablets of the Law" by Hermensz van Rijn Rembrandt (1606–69), Dahlem Staatliche Gemaldegalerie, Berlin, 34 "Saul Listening to David Playing the Harp" by Erasmus Quellinus (1607–78), Museum of Fine Arts, Budapest, 41(t) " The Jewish Marriage" by Ilex Bellers (20th century), Private Collection; British Library, Oriental & India Office Collections, pp12,13(c), 40; Camera Press, p31(t) (Y Braun); Circa Photo Library, pp25(t), 43 (Barrie Searle); Kuperard Ltd, p20; Hulton Deutsch Collection, p27(br); Israeli Post Office, Philatetic Service, p34(r); Henry Jacobs, p35(b); Michael Le Poer Trench, p13(b); Rony Oren, *The Animated Haggadah*, Scopus Films (London) Ltd, p33(t) (Trevor Clifford); Zev Radovan, Jerusalem, pp27(bl), 31(b), 32, 37; Peter Sanders Photography, p36; Traditions Mail Order, endpapers (Trevor Clifford), 39(t) from the original in the Israeli Museum (Jeffrey Gendler); Stewart Weir, pp17(br), 23, 24, 25(b), 38, 39(b); Westhill RE Centre, pp15(r), 16, 17(t), 30; Zefa Pictures, pp17(bl),18, 19, 21(t), 22, 27, 28, 29(b), 35(t).

Printed in Hong Kong by Wing King Tong

A CIP record for this book
is available from the Library of Congress, Washington, D.C.

Peter Bedrick Books and the swan logo are trademarks of Peter Bedrick Books Inc.

ISBN: 0-87226-386-X

Endpapers: This hand-painted silk Sabbath cloth shows the seven foods harvested at Sukkot time: wheat, barley, grapes, olives, pomegranates, dates and figs.
(by Yair Emanuel, Emanuel Studio, Jerusalem)

99 98 97 96 1 2 3 4

WHAT·DO·WE·KNOW
ABOUT
JUDAISM·?

DOREEN FINE

PETER BEDRICK BOOKS

NEW YORK

j296
FIN

Published by
Peter Bedrick Books
2112 Broadway
New York, NY 10023

© Macdonald Young Books Ltd 1995

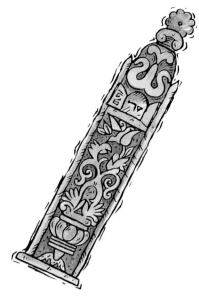

Published by agreement with Macdonald Young Books Ltd, England

Designer and illustrator: Celia Hart
Commissioning editor: Debbie Fox
Editors: Caroline Arthur, Lesley Taylor
Picture research: Jane Taylor
Consultant: Laurie Rosenberg, Executive Director of Education, Board of
Deputies of British Jews

Photograph acknowledgements: Front and back cover: Stewart Weir; Andes
Press Agency, pp8, 41(b) (Carlos Reyes-Manzo); Architectural Association,
p21(b) (John Ross); MS Kennicott 1 Folio 305ᴿ·, Bodleian Library Oxford;
Anat Rotem-Braun, Jerusalem, pp15(l), 29(t), 31(c); Werner Braun,
Jerusalem, p33(b); Bridgeman Art Library, pp13(t) Giraudon/ "Jacob's
Dream" by Ludovico Cardi da Cigoli (1559–1613), Musée des Beaux-Arts,
Nancy, 14 "Moses and the Tablets of the Law" by Hermensz
van Rijn Rembrandt (1606–69), Dahlem Staatliche Gemaldegalerie, Berlin,
34 "Saul Listening to David Playing the Harp" by Erasmus Quellinus
(1607–78), Museum of Fine Arts, Budapest, 41(t) " The Jewish Marriage"
by Ilex Bellers (20th century), Private Collection; British Library, Oriental &
India Office Collections, pp12,13(c), 40; Camera Press, p31(t) (Y Braun);
Circa Photo Library, pp25(t), 43 (Barrie Searle); Kuperard Ltd, p20;
Hulton Deutsch Collection, p27(br); Israeli Post Office, Philatetic Service,
p34(r); Henry Jacobs, p35(b); Michael Le Poer Trench, p13(b); Rony Oren,
The Animated Haggadah, Scopus Films (London) Ltd, p33(t) (Trevor
Clifford); Zev Radovan, Jerusalem, pp27(bl), 31(b), 32, 37; Peter Sanders
Photography, p36; Traditions Mail Order,
endpapers (Trevor Clifford), 39(t) from the original in the Israeli Museum
(Jeffrey Gendler); Stewart Weir, pp17(br), 23, 24, 25(b), 38, 39(b); Westhill
RE Centre, pp15(r), 16, 17(t), 30; Zefa Pictures, pp17(bl),18, 19, 21(t), 22,
27, 28, 29(b), 35(t).

Printed in Hong Kong by Wing King Tong

A CIP record for this book
is available from the Library of Congress, Washington, D.C.

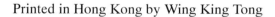

ISBN: 0-87226-386-X

Endpapers: This hand-painted silk Sabbath cloth
shows the seven foods harvested at Sukkot time:
wheat, barley, grapes, olives, pomegranates, dates
and figs.
(by Yair Emanuel, Emanuel Studio, Jerusalem)

99 98 97 96 1 2 3 4

· CONTENTS ·

WHO·ARE·THE·JEWS?

In the beginning, Abraham, the founder of the Jewish religion, was a wandering herdsman overseeing flocks of sheep and goats. The first Jews were a tribal people who moved about in the area that today includes Israel, Jordan, Syria and northern Iraq. Today Jews live in all parts of the world and are of many nationalities. How then is a Jew defined? The religious definition is that a person is Jewish only if his or her mother is Jewish. However, Reform Judaism will recognize as Jewish the child of a Jewish father and a non-Jewish mother if that child is raised as a Jew and publicly accepts Judaism. It is also possible to become Jewish by conversion. Because Judaism is a way of life as well as a religion, there are non-observant Jews who consider themselves Jewish because of their identification with Jewish history and culture. As a result of their dispersion across the globe, Jews live a variety of lifestyles. While a majority live in urban areas, there are Jews in Israel who live in collective farms called a *kibbutz*, that are in remote areas. There are Jewish farmers as well as doctors, Jewish policemen as well as businessmen, Jewish fisherman as well as lawyers. There are poor Jews as well as rich Jews, with the majority in-between.

KIBBUTZ

Some Jews live isolated from any other Jews on remote farms, or in small towns and villages far away from centers of Jewish population. In Israel, many Jews live in communal farm villages. One type of farm village is known as a *kibbutz*. The kibbutz children live together, go to school together, work together and play together, as you can see in the photograph on the left. Their parents take turns at doing all the work in the kibbutz. This may be on the farm or in the houses, the kitchen or the laundry. They also take turns in managing the kibbutz.

THE JEWISH WORLD POPULATION

It is estimated that there are 13-15 million Jews in the world. In the United Sates there are about 6 million Jews (2.5% of the US population). There are about 3 million in the former Soviet Union and other Eastern European countries, and approximately 1 million Jews in western Europe and Scandinavia, with most in Great Britain (320,000) and in France (530,000). In Israel the Jewish population is 3.5 million.

JEWISH RELIGIOUS DENOMINATIONS

With the end of the Jewish state in 135 CE, the dispersion of the Jews throughout the Mediterranean world and Europe resulted in the development of two distinct traditions: the Sephardic and the Ashkenazic. The Sephardic Jews lived in Islamic communities in Spain, North Africa and the Middle East. The Ashkenazic Jews lived in Christian communities in both western and eastern Europe. The majority of the world's Jews in the 20th century are Ashkenazic, but in Israel the mixture is 50-50. The distinctions between Sephardic and Ashkenazic Jews are ones of traditions relating to food and synagogue melodies, and not ones of doctrine or faith.

In the United States, there is a small Sephardic community, but most American Jews are of European ancestry and belong to one of the following denominations.

Hasidic Judaism, sometimes called Ultra-Orthodoxy, is centered on a single religious leader, the Rebbe, who interprets religious law for his followers. Hasidic Jews are recognizable by their distinctive appearance and dress which reflects the 18th-century origins of Hasidism in rural Poland.

Reform Judaism originated in Germany in the early 19th century. The first Reform congregation in the US was organized in Charleston, SC in 1824. Reform Judaism is an effort to modernize ritual in the following ways:
   1. Replace portions of the Hebrew synagogue service with prayers in English
   2. Introduce music into the service with a choir and organ.
   3. Permit men and women to sit together in the synagogue.
   4. Abandon the biblical dietary laws.
Philosophically, Reform believes in the interpretation of the Jewish tradition on the basis of individual conscience. It is estimated that more than 40 percent of American Jews are Reform Jews.

Orthodox Judaism was a reaction to Reform Judaism. Prior to the Reform movement, all Jews observed a similar ritual and a similar prayerbook which was entirely in Hebrew. Orthodox Jews observed the tradition as stated, "...regardless of how modern thought or personal conscience may view the practice in question." It is estimated that about 6 percent of American Jews are Orthodox.

Conservative Judaism also developed as a reaction to Reform by those who considered Reform too extreme, and would result in the disappearance of American Judaism. Conservative Judaism was organized in 1885 in New York City, and began with the dedication there of the Jewish Theological Seminary in 1887. Conservative Judaism accepted the reforms of men and women sitting together, and the use of organ music, but it refused to abandon the traditional Sabbath worship conducted mainly in Hebrew, and it adhered to the biblical dietary laws. The ordination of women as rabbis in the 1980's and after has resulted in some divisions within the movement. "In 1990, approximately 40 percent of North America Jews claimed to be Conservative, but the number was shrinking from what it had been ten years earlier."

[The source for some of the material quoted above, comes from "What Is A Jew?" by Rabbi Morris N. Kertzer, revised by Rabbi Lawrence A. Hoffman. Collier Books, Macmillan Publishing Co., 1993, pages 7-14.]

TIMELINE

BCE is an abbreviation of Before the Common Era and CE is an abbreviation of the Common Era. The Common Era is where time is measured before or after what is believed to be the birth year of Jesus. The Jewish calendar is dated from the supposed creation of the world. According to the Jewish calendar, the year 1996 CE is the year 5756/57. CA is an abbreviation of *circa* which means approximately.

CA 2000-1700 BCE The era of the Patriarchs, Abraham, Issac and Jacob.	**CA 1250-1200 BCE** The era of Moses, the Exodus from Egypt which is celebrated at the Passover seder; the giving of the Ten	Commandments. **1028-1013 BCE** Saul is the first King of Israel. **1013-1006 BCE** David, King of Judah.	**1006-973 BCE** David, King of all Israel. **973-933 BCE** Solomon, David's son, King of Israel. Dedicates the First Temple at Jerusalem 953 BCE.	**933 BCE** After the death of Solomon, the kingdom is divided into Judah in the South and Israel in the North.	**722 BCE** Northern Kingdom conquered by Assyria. **587 BCE** Southern kingdom conquered by Babylonians under Nebchadnezzar. Solomon's Temple

Noah's Ark

The Tablets of the Law

638 CE Muslim conquest of Jerusalem; Jews permitted to return to Judea.	**CA 600 CE** Completion of the "Babylonian" Talmud. **570-632 CE** Muhammad, the Prophet, founder of Islam.	**381 CE** Christianity established as the state religion of the Roman Empire. **CA 500 CE** Completion of the "Jerusalem" Talmud.	**313 CE.** By the edict of toleration issued at Milan, the Emperor Constantine suspends persecution of Christians.	**CA 200 CE** The *Mishna*, the oral law, later part of the Talmud, is edited and written down.	**132-134 CE** Second war with Rome. Jerusalem destroyed and Jews forbidden to live there.
1096 CE Crusader knights destroy many Jewish communities on their way to the Holy Land.					
1492 CE Christian conquest of Spain completed; Jews forced to convert or flee. **1654 CE** Jews settle in New Amsterdam, later New York.	**1818 CE** First reform synagogue established in Hamburg, Germany. **1848 CE** First large-scale emigration of German Jews to the US.	**1881-1905 CE** More than one million Jewish refugees arrive in America from Eastern Europe.	**1882 CE** Eliezer Ben-Jehuda settles in Palestine where he advocates the use of Hebrew not only for prayer and study, but as the everyday language.	**1886 CE** Sabato Morais opens the Jewish Theological Seminary in New York City.	**1897 CE** The First Zionist Congress, under the leadership of Theodore Herzl, agrees to "seek to establish a home for the Jewish people in Palestine."

is destroyed, and the Israelites sent into exile. **538 BCE** First return of exiles from Babylon.	**515 BCE** Dedication of the Second Temple. **400 BCE** The Torah is edited into its final form.	**334 BCE** Alexander the Great conquers the Persian Empire including Palestine. Alexander dies in 323 BCE.	**285-247 BCE** The Bible is translated into Greek by 70 scholars in Alexandria, Egypt. **165 BCE** The Temple is rededicated after the successful revolt of the
			Maccabees against Greek rule, commemorated in the festival of Chanukkah.
30 CE Crucifixion of Jesus and the beginning of Christian era. **66-73 CE** War with Rome; destruction of the Second Temple in 70 CE.	**CA 4** Birth of Jesus. **6 CE** Romans assume direct rule of Judea.	**37-34 BCE** Herod "the Great" as tributary King of Judea enlarges the Temple to its greatest magnificence.	**63 BCE** Pompey captures Jerusalem marking the beginning of Roman rule in Palestine.
1902-14 CE Zionist colonies established in Palestine.	**1917 CE** The British Foreign Secretary, Arthur Balfour, issues a declaration that the British Government views with favor the establishment in Palestine of a national home for the Jewish people.	**1939-1945 CE** Destruction of European Jews by the Nazis and those who helped them. **1948 CE** State of Israel founded.	**1969 CE** Golda Meir becomes Prime Minister. **1979 CE** Egyptian-Israeli agreement signed.

King David's lyre

Theodore Herzl

THE STATE OF ISRAEL

From 69 CE, for over 1,800 years, Jews have prayed daily for the re-establishment of Israel as the Jewish homeland and for the rebuilding of the Temple.

After the Second World War, most Jews in the world had been either killed by the Nazis or forced to leave their countries, or were living in societies that either banned Judaism or persecuted them for being Jews.

In 1947, the United Nations, an organization set up to establish world peace, recommended that Palestine be split into two separate states, Jewish and Arab. This was to give a safe haven to the displaced and unwanted Jews of the world. On 14 May 1948, the State of Israel was born.

Shield of David

MAGEN DAVID

The six-pointed star, the 'Shield of David', or the 'Seal of Solomon' as it was sometimes known, has been used as a particularly Jewish symbol since the late Middle Ages. However, it was used in Christian and Moslem culture as well as in earlier times. It was later adopted by the Zionist movement and for the national flag of Israel.

Jews believe that Judaism began when Abram, the father of the Jewish religion, began to worship one God instead of many idols as his father had done. According to the Torah, Abram was born in 1813 BCE and married Sarai. They set out on a journey led by God. Abram entered into a covenant or agreement with God. He promised to be faithful to God and to teach his laws to the world. To mark the covenant, Abram circumcised himself. God changed the names of the couple to Abraham and Sarah (the extra 'h' is a symbol for God). He promised that they would have a son. He said that their descendants would be as many as the stars in the sky and they would inherit the Land of Israel.

CANAANITE IDOLS

The people of the land of Canaan, where Abraham was born, worshiped idols – statues made of clay, stone or bronze. They believed that if they pleased the idols they would be granted their wishes, such as strength, victory in battle or a good harvest. To gain good fortune from the idols, people gave them offerings. Astarte, who is pictured below, was a well-known goddess. Baal was the most famous god.

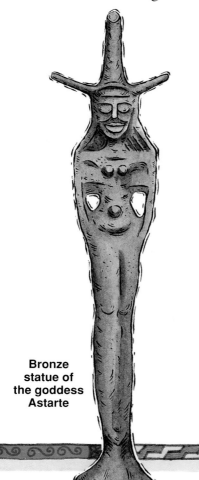

Bronze statue of the goddess Astarte

ABRAHAM AND ISAAC

The painting above shows a famous scene from the story of Abraham. To test Abraham's character, God ordered Abraham to sacrifice Isaac, his favorite son, on Mount Moriah. Abraham obeyed, but God sent an angel to stop him. To show his thanks, Abraham looked around for a suitable offering to God. He found a ram caught in a bush (in the lower right of the painting).

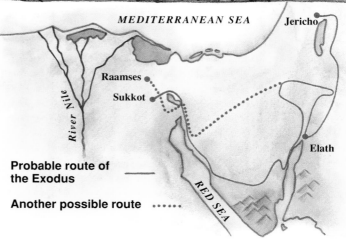

MEDITERRANEAN SEA
Jericho
Raamses
Sukkot
River Nile
Elath
RED SEA

Probable route of the Exodus ——

Another possible route ······

The route the Israelites took when going from Egypt to Israel

THE EXODUS

After Joseph's death, a new pharaoh made the Israelites into slaves. He would not let them worship their own God, and drowned their baby boys in the River Nile. God appointed a new leader, Moses, and sent ten plagues to show Pharaoh his anger. After Pharaoh had let the Israelites leave Egypt, he chased after them. So as a punishment, God drowned Pharaoh's army in the Red Sea (pictured below).

JACOB'S DREAM

Jacob was Abraham's grandson. When he was a young man, he dreamed of a ladder going down from Earth up to Heaven, with angels going up and down, as shown in the painting above. In the dream, God promised to protect Jacob wherever he went. May years later, Jacob had another dream, of a night-long struggle with a mysterious being, after which Jacob was renamed Israel, meaning "he who wrestles with God."

JOSEPH

Joseph was Jacob's favorite son. Jacob gave him a special coat. Joseph was sold into slavery by his brothers. Later, he rose to power in Egypt because God told him the meaning of Pharaoh's – the king's – dreams. This popular story has been made into a modern musical. Here, Philip Schofield plays Joseph in *Joseph and the Amazing Technicolour Dreamcoat.*

 THE CHILDREN OF ISRAEL

Abraham and Sarah had one son, Isaac. Isaac and Rebekkah had twins, Jacob and Esau. Jacob married four women: Leah and Rachel, and their maids, Bilhah and Zilpah. Jacob's sons became the fathers of the Twelve Tribes of Israel. Leah's sons were Reuben, Simeon, Levi, Judah, Issachar and Zebulun. Rachel's sons were Joseph and Benjamin. Zilpah's sons were Gad and Asher, and Bilhah's were Dan and Naphtali.

WHAT·DO ·JEWS· BELIEVE?

There is a wide range of Jewish beliefs. Reformed Jews believe that being Jewish gives them a common culture, while Orthodox Jews try to keep all the laws and customs commanded by the Torah. The basic Jewish religious belief is in the existence of one, eternal, invisible God. The Jews also believe they were chosen to receive God's *Torah* – the first part of the *Tanakh* (the Jewish bible). They believe that by looking at its many meanings, and by living according to its laws, they can spread justice throughout the world. At the right time, they believe that the Messiah will come to bring this perfect world. Reward for good deeds will largely be granted in the World to Come (Heaven).

THE TABLETS OF THE LAW

Jews believe that seven weeks after the Israelites left Egypt, God chose them to receive the Torah. Moses climbed Mount Sinai to hear the Torah and bring the Commandments back to the people, carved into stone tablets. In this painting, Moses is holding the second tablet in front, which shows Commandments six to ten. The stone tablets were kept in a special gold box – the Ark – inside a magnificent tent – the Tabernacle – in the Wilderness.

 ## THE TEN COMMANDMENTS

1 I am the Lord your God, who has brought you out of the land of Egypt, out of the house of bondage. You shall have no other gods before me.
2 You shall not make any graven image.
3 You shall not take the name of the Lord your God in vain.
4 Remember the Sabbath Day, to keep it holy.
5 Honor your father and mother.
6 You shall not kill.
7 You shall not not commit adultery.
8 You shall not steal.
9 You shall not bear false witness against your neighbor.
10 You shall not covet your neighbor's property.

THE SIX DAYS OF CREATION

First Day

The Jews believe that on the first day of the Creation of the World, God made night and day. Earth and Heaven were created on the second day, and seas and land and everything that grows from the ground on the third day. On the fourth day, the Sun, Moon and stars were created, and on the fifth day, the fish and birds. On the sixth day, God made all land animals and, finally, people. On the seventh day, God rested.

Sixth Day

Second Day

Fifth Day

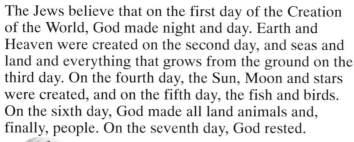

Third Day

Fourth Day

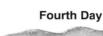

ORTHODOX JEWS

Many Jews carry out even everyday activities in special ways, believing that this brings them closer to God. The men in the photograph are immersing cooking pots in water in preparation for Passover. Water is a symbol for purity in Judaism and is used in other ceremonies. People sometimes immerse themselves in 'living water' – rain, river or sea water – in a special pool called a *mikveh*. A convert to Judaism uses the mikveh as a symbol to show re-birth as a Jew. The long side-curls and beards worn by the men on the left show their interpretation of certain Biblical commandments.

WOMAN RABBI

Reformed Jews believe that laws can be changed to suit modern times. One recent change states that men and women should be equal in every area of Jewish practice. Reform Judaism accepts women as rabbis with the authority to fulfill all religious duties.

· HOW · DO · JEWISH · FAMILIES · LIVE ? ·

Judaism is observed in the home as well as the synagogue. There are religious rituals that are observed exclusively in the home, such as *kashrut*, the preparation of food so that it is ritually acceptable, i.e. kosher. Foods containing milk are never mixed with meat, nor eaten at the same meal. The weekly Sabbath is observed in the home, and begins with a woman of the house lighting Sabbath candles. Observant Jews recite blessings before eating over wine, bread and other foods.

MEZUZAH

Many Jewish homes have a *mezuzah* fixed to the frame of most doors in the house. The mezuzah is a handwritten parchment scroll with the words of the *Shema* prayer – the most important Jewish prayer, proclaiming the oneness of God. Some families have a special celebration when they move to a new house and fix the mezuzah to the front door. Usually the mezuzah is rolled up inside a beautiful case, like the one in the drawing.

Mezuzah

CHARITY BOX

Charity is a basic Jewish belief and many Jewish homes have a charity box. Children are often given money to put in the box on Friday, in honor of Sabbath. Adults in the family also put in money regularly. The money from the box on the right went to buy clothes for people who had none.

Charity box

Kosher food guide

KOSHER FOOD GUIDE

Many Jewish families use a food guide to help make sure that any foods they buy or eat outside the home are strictly kosher. Some guides, like the one in the picture, give advice about medicines and kosher cooking as well.

A KOSHER KITCHEN

According to the rules of *kashrut* – kosher eating – milk and all other dairy products, such as cheese, may not be cooked or eaten with meat. In the kosher kitchen above, meat meals are cooked and washed up with red equipment, and foods containing milk products with blue equipment. There are even separate sinks and dishwashers for milk and meat equipment.

 KEEPING KOSHER

The rules for kosher animals, birds and fish come directly from the Torah.

Kosher fish include:
plaice, salmon, sardines, trout, herring, sole and cod.

Kosher animals include:
cows, sheep, goats and deer.

Kosher birds include:
chickens, ducks, geese and turkeys.

Animals and birds must be killed by a special method, called *Shechitah*.

THE FAMILY

Some Jews consider large families a blessing and feel they are part of one large Jewish family. A family outing, as in the photograph, is one way of being together. Many Jewish ceremonies and rituals involve not only parents but children and other members of the family, such as grandparents.

WASHING BEFORE A MEAL

The picture above shows a young girl being taught the proper way to wash her hands before a meal. Jewish children begin taking part in rituals and ceremonies from the age of three and many aspects of the Jewish way of life are learned in the home.

WHAT·ARE THE·MOST IMPORTANT ·TIMES·IN· ·A·JEW'S· ·LIFE?·

The four most important stages in Jewish life are birth, reaching adulthood, marriage and death. All of these are marked by religious ceremonies, some of which are unchanged since they were first commanded in the Torah. During these ceremonies the family and community say thank you to God. They also say that they believe in God and accept God's will. All Jewish ceremonies, such as circumcision and naming ceremonies for boys, naming ceremonies for girls, weddings, deaths and memorial services, enable people to share their happiness or sorrow. They can carry out religious duties and feel part of a warm and caring community.

JEWISH NAMES

As well as a first name and a surname, such as Claire Jones, religious Jews also have a Jewish name. In a Jewish name, people are known by their first names, followed by 'son of' or 'daughter of' their parents' first names. Sometimes only the father's name is used and sometimes only the mother's. Some Jews use both parents' names at all times. So if a boy's first name is David, his mother is Ruth and his father is Aaron, he is David ben (son of) Aaron, or David ben Ruth, or David ben Aaron and Ruth. David's sister, Esther, would be Esther bat (daughter of) Aaron, or Esther bat Ruth, or Esther bat Aaron and Ruth.

CIRCUMCISION AND NAMING

When he is eight days old, a boy is circumcised. This is to show his entry into the covenant of Abraham. He is given his Jewish name and everyone prays that he should be blessed with Torah study, marriage and good deeds.

A girl may be named by her father in a synagogue immediately after birth, or at a baby-naming ceremony.

Cushion used at a circumcision ceremony

BAR MITZVAH

When a boy reaches 13, he becomes *Bar Mitzvah*. This means that he takes on all the religious and legal obligations of an adult. For an Orthodox boy, he should wear *tefillin* – two small black leather boxes with leather straps – each weekday morning, as the boy in the photograph on the left is learning to do. Bar Mitzvah is celebrated in many communities by calling a boy up to the Torah reading on Sabbath morning, which is an adult privilege. Usually the Bar Mitzvah will read part or all of the morning's Torah reading and say the blessings for the first time. In celebration, the family often gives a *kiddush* – a reception – in the synagogue and a festive meal at home.

BAT MITZVAH

A 12-year-old girl celebrates becoming *Bat Mitzvah*. In Reformed communities, she may learn to read from the Torah, as in the photograph on the right. Orthodox girls may celebrate their Bat Mitzvah in the synagogue, at home, at school, or in a Sunday afternoon ceremony.

MARRIAGE

Jewish weddings, more than any other Jewish ceremony, vary around the world. They can be informal, outdoor ceremonies, or very formal synagogue ceremonies as shown in the photograph below. All weddings have the *chuppah* – a canopy – which is a symbol for the couple's new home, and a veil is worn over the bride's face. A glass is broken by the groom as a reminder of the destruction of the two Temples.

Memorial candle

Ceremonial wedding ring

DEATH AND MOURNING

The bodies of Orthodox Jews are always buried, but other Jewish denominations allow cremation. After the funeral, the parents, husband or wife, sisters, brothers or children of the dead person observe the *shivah* – a seven-day mourning period. They sit on low chairs all day, while family and friends visit to pray with them, comfort them and bring them food. On the anniversary of the death, every year, a memorial candle is lit and special prayers are said.

WHERE·DO ·JEWS· ·PRAY?·

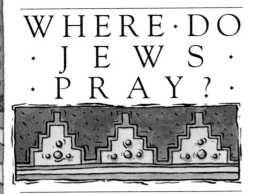

Jews pray anywhere and everywhere! Every action and occasion is an opportunity for them to pray. Whenever Jews eat or drink, put on new clothes, hear bad news, go to bed or get up, there is a suitable blessing to say. If Jews go on a long journey, there is a prayer to say. If they are not sure what prayer to say, in a place where something terrible has happened, or where something wonderful has happened, they are encouraged to make up their own prayers. In the synagogue, there are prayers to say for every occasion.

PRAYING IN BED

This boy in the photograph is saying the bedtime prayers. He is covering his eyes to help him concentrate on the Shema prayer. He will also ask God and the most important angels, the archangels Michael, Gabriel, Uriel and Raphael, to guard him while he sleeps.

 ## TIMES FOR PRAYER

Some Jewish prayers, such as the morning, afternoon and evening prayers, need to be said at fixed times, wherever you are. Orthodox Jewish men of 13 years and over are always supposed to say these prayers. Women traditionally had to look after the home and children and could not be expected to stop everything to pray. Therefore there are fewer prayers that they must say. Many Reformed Jews only say these prayers when they are in the synagogue, on Sabbath or during the festivals.

THE SYNAGOGUE IN DJERBA

Jews have been praying in synagogues since the time of the first Temple (953 BCE). This synagogue in Tunisia is very old. It is in the style of Arab buildings. The men are praying at tables and benches and are wearing the traditional clothes of Jews of Arab lands, such as the red hat called a *fez*.

ORTHODOX AND REFORMED SYNAGOGUES

The main difference between an Orthodox and a Reformed synagogue is that in Reformed synagogues men and women sit together for prayer and in Orthodox synagogues they are separated. Sometimes women sit behind a screen at the same level as the men; sometimes they sit upstairs in a balcony. Below are examples of the inside of an Orthodox synagogue and an American Reformed synagogue.

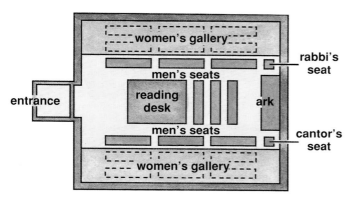

Orthodox synagogue

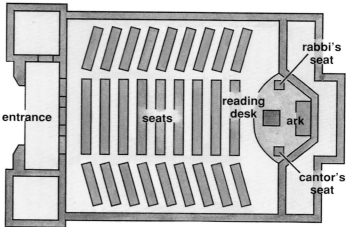

Reformed synagogue

THE BETH SHALOM SYNAGOGUE

This spectacular synagogue was designed by the famous architect Frank Lloyd Wright in 1959. It was built for the congregation at Elkins Park, Philadelphia, USA. Modern synagogues like this are a sign that Judaism is thriving in the 20th century. The synagogue is the center of a Jewish community. A modern synagogue is not only a place of prayer and study, but also houses social, leisure and welfare services for members, friends and visitors.

HOW · DO · JEWS · PRAY?

From about the age of three, Jews are encouraged to bring God into all activities by saying short prayers such as *berachot* – blessings – which are for every occasion. Then there are set prayer services, which Orthodox Jewish men are obliged to say three times each day, in Hebrew. Prayers are silent, chanted aloud, or sung. Many Reformed Jews have shortened these, and say them only in the synagogue on Friday nights, Sabbath mornings and special occasions. They pray in a mixture of Hebrew and the local language. Normally, Jews pray sitting or standing, though some prayers should be said when in bed, like the bedtime Shema.

PRAYING IN A SYNAGOGUE

Prayers in the synagogue can be led by the Rabbi, the Cantor – who is a professional prayer leader – or an ordinary person. In an Orthodox synagogue, prayers can be led only by men, or boys of thirteen years or over. In the photograph above, you can see the Cantor, who has his back to the congregation and is chanting a prayer while the Torah scrolls are taken out of the Holy Ark. The Rabbi is on the far right of the photograph. In many Reformed synagogues, prayers can also be led by women, and men and women sit together.

SAYING THE MORNING SERVICE

In the photograph on the right, an Orthodox Jewish man is saying the weekday morning service. He is wearing a small skull cap, called a *yarmulke* or *kippah*; a prayer shawl, called a *tallit*, and *tefillin*. The two boxes of the tefillin are worn on the head and next to the heart, and they contain holy prayers. This is to remind the wearer each day of the important message of the Shema prayer.

 ## THE SHEMA PRAYER

Listen Israel, the Lord is our God, the Lord is one. Let the name of his magnificent kingdom be blessed for ever and ever.

You shall love the Lord your God with all your heart, with all your soul and with everything you have. Let these words, which I command you today, be on your heart. Teach them carefully to your children. Speak of them when you are sitting at home and when you are traveling, when you go to bed and when you get up. Tie them on your arm as a sign and as tefillin between your eyes. Write them on the doorposts of your house and on your gateposts.

PRAYING AT MEALTIMES

Before lunch, these children in a Jewish school wash their hands in a special way, as shown in the photograph on page 17. They say one short blessing. They then say another blessing, after which they eat a piece of bread and then their meal. After lunch, as in this photograph, the children say and sing *Birkat Hamazon* – the Blessings after Meals – from books that are written in Hebrew.

BLESSING THE CHILDREN

Before the meal on Fridays and on festival evenings, parents bless their children, praying that God will help them and look after them. Girls are blessed with the good qualities of the 'Four Mothers' of the Jewish people – Sarah, Rebekkah, Rachel and Leah. Boys are blessed with Jacob's blessing for his grandsons, Ephraim and Menasseh.

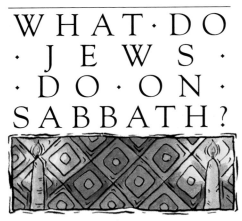

WHAT·DO ·JEWS· ·DO·ON· SABBATH?

On Friday night, a little before sunset, Sabbath, the day of rest, begins. It lasts until sundown on Saturday night. Many Jews put aside all weekday activities and worries. They prepare their homes as if for a royal visitor – the Sabbath Queen – and put on their best clothes. They also light candles, and serve the best food they can afford at a beautifully set table. Often guests are invited to share meals, songs, stories, prayers and Torah learning. Attending the synagogue, visits to friends, walks and study activities all add to the spirit of the day.

Havdalah candle

LIGHTING CANDLES

Sabbath enters the Jewish home with the lighting of at least two candles that symbolize joy and holiness, and the saying of a blessing. Some families add another candle for each child. As you can see in the photograph, whoever lights the candles – often mothers and daughters – welcomes in Sabbath with a gesture over the candles; they then cover their eyes to say the blessing.

 ACTIVITIES FORBIDDEN ON SABBATH

There were 39 types of activity that were carried out when building the Tabernacle in the wilderness, but which had to stop on Sabbath, to make it a day of complete rest. Today, this same law means that Orthodox Jews don't do any of the following once Sabbath has begun:

cook; light a fire; switch on electrical equipment; write; watch television; play musical instruments; travel in a car, bus, boat, train or airplane, or ride a bicycle or motorcycle. In order to follow the law, food, light and heat are all prepared before Sabbath to last the whole day.

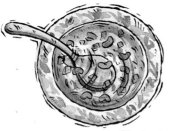
Cholent
(hamim)

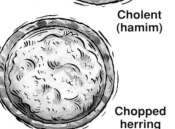
Chopped
herring

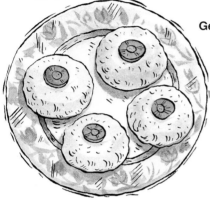
Gefilte fish

Chopped
liver

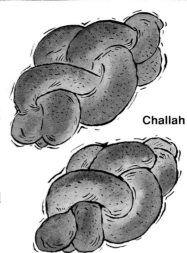
Challah

FOOD FOR SABBATH

At dinner on Friday night and Sabbath lunch, the meal starts with blessings over wine and two *challah* – traditional loaves of bread. Jews were often very poor and many of the traditional recipes were clever ways of making a little meat or fish feed a lot of people! Examples are liver, chopped with egg and onion, and *gefilte* fish (a type of fishcake). *Cholent*, or *hamim*, is meat stewed with onions, potatoes and beans on a low heat over Friday night and Sabbath morning so that there will be a hot meal for lunch.

READING THE TORAH

Each Sabbath is known by the name of that week's Torah reading. The Torah reading is the central part of the morning service. The Torah scroll, the most holy object in Judaism, is taken to the *bimah* – the reading desk on the stage – in a stately procession. Reading from the Torah, as the rabbi in the photograph on the right is doing, is a special skill. It is a great honor to read it, or to be called to stand on the bimah to hear a section read.

HAVDALAH

Just as the arrival of Sabbath is celebrated, so is its departure, with prayer and ceremony. When three stars can be seen in the sky, Sabbath is over for another week and *Havdalah* (the separation) is celebrated. Havdalah, which separates the holiness of Sabbath from the rest of the week, is performed with blessings over wine, spices and a plaited candle, as the photograph on the left shows. Children eagerly await their turn to hold the candle and to sniff the sweet-smelling spices.

·HOW·DOES· THE·JEWISH CALENDAR ·WORK?·

The Jewish calendar has 12 months which run according to the Moon, rather than the Sun, as the civil calendar does. Each Jewish month has either 29 or 30 days and every Jewish year is about 11 days shorter than a civil year. The Jewish calendar must keep up with the civil year, or all the festivals would eventually end up in the wrong seasons. (Jewish festivals are celebrated on fixed dates.) To do this, the calendar has leap years, with an extra month of Adar in January–February. The normal month of Adar (February–March) is then called Adar 2. There are seven leap years every 19 years. There is a celebration, *Rosh Chodesh*, for the beginning of each month.

THE JEWISH CALENDAR

Tishrei (September–October)

Rosh Hashanah (2 days)
Yom Kippur (1 day)
Sukkot (7 days)
Shemini Atzeret (1day)
Simchat Torah (1 day)

Cheshvan (October–November)
There are no festivals in Cheshvan.
It is sometimes known as MarCheshvan or 'bitter Cheshvan' for this reason.

Kislev (November–December)   Chanukkah (8 days)

Tevet (December–January)   Chanukkah

Shevat (January–February)   Tu Bishvat (1 day)
(New Year for Trees)

Adar (February–March)   Purim (1 day)

Nisan (March–April)

Pesach (7–8 days)
Yom HaSho'ah (1 day)
(Remembrance of the Holocaust)

Iyyar (April–May)

Yom Ha'Atsma'ut (1 day)
(Israel's Independence Day)
Lag baOmer (1 day)

Sivan (May–June)   Shavuot (1–2 days)

Tammuz (June–July)   Fast of Tammuz

Av (July–August)   Tishah b'Av (1 day)
(Day of Mourning)

Elul (August–September)   Preparations for Rosh Hashanah

There are no festivals in Elul.

ROSH HASHANAH AND YOM KIPPUR

The Jewish New Year, *Rosh Hashanah*, is on 1 and 2 Tishrei (September-October). *Yom Kippur,* a 25-hour fast and the most solemn festival, is on 10 Tishrei. The first ten days of Tishrei, which include these two festivals, are known as the Ten Days of Penitence. During this period, Jews apologize to people and to God for wrongdoings. They pray for forgiveness and a new start in life. The *shofar* or ram's horn is blown to wake up the conscience, as in the photograph on the left. People send each other New Year cards, wishing a happy, healthy and sweet year. Some wear white clothes and use white material for all cloths and hangings in the synagogue, as a symbol of purity and newness. Bread and apple are dipped in honey, to symbolize sweetness, and honey cake is a traditional treat.

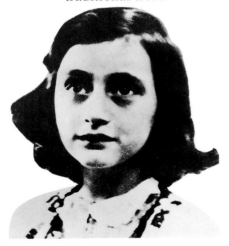

YOM HA'ATSMA'UT

Israel's Independence Day is the only festival that has been added to the calendar for hundreds of years. The State of Israel was created by the United Nations on May 14, 1948 CE. In Israel this date is celebrated as a national holiday, and it is a festival in Jewish communities throughout the world. Celebrations include services of thanksgiving and parties with Israeli folksinging.

YOM HASHO'AH

On 27 *Nisan*, Jews all over the world hold ceremonies honoring the memory of the six million Jews killed by the Nazis, before and during the Second World War, from 1939 to 1945 CE. Many Jewish families and whole towns of Jews were completely destroyed. One of the most famous victims was Anne Frank photographed above. Her diary has been read by millions of people.

· W H A T · ARE · THE · THREE · PILGRIM · FESTIVALS?

When the Temple was standing, Jews made a pilgrimage to Jerusalem to make offerings on the three festivals of *Pesach*, *Shavuot* and *Sukkot*. Jews who lived outside Israel had to sell part of their crops and send the money to buy offerings and to help in the upkeep of the Temple and the priests. Pesach, or Passover, is the festival that celebrates the Exodus from Egypt. A lamb was offered at the Temple. At Shavuot, some of the first produce of each harvest had to be offered at the Temple. Sukkot is the festival of the end of the harvest. Harvest offerings were made at the Temple. Now there is no Temple, Jews celebrate these festivals at home and in the synagogue.

PESACH (PASSOVER)
This beautiful plate is an example of those that are used at Passover Seder services in Jewish homes. The pictures around the rim are the Ten Plagues suffered by the Egyptians. The bone is a symbol of the Passover lamb, and the burned egg symbolizes the festival offering. Both were offered at the Temple. Next to the bone is bitter horseradish, symbolizing the bitter life under the Egyptians. Next to the egg is *charoset*, a spicy nut mixture which symbolizes the mortar for building the pyramids. Below that is salt-water, for the tears of the Israelites, and lastly green vegetables. All are eaten, or talked about, in a special order. One of the most important ingredients of the service is *matzo* or unleavened bread. This was the bread of the poor people. The Israelites ate this in Egypt and took it with them when they left.

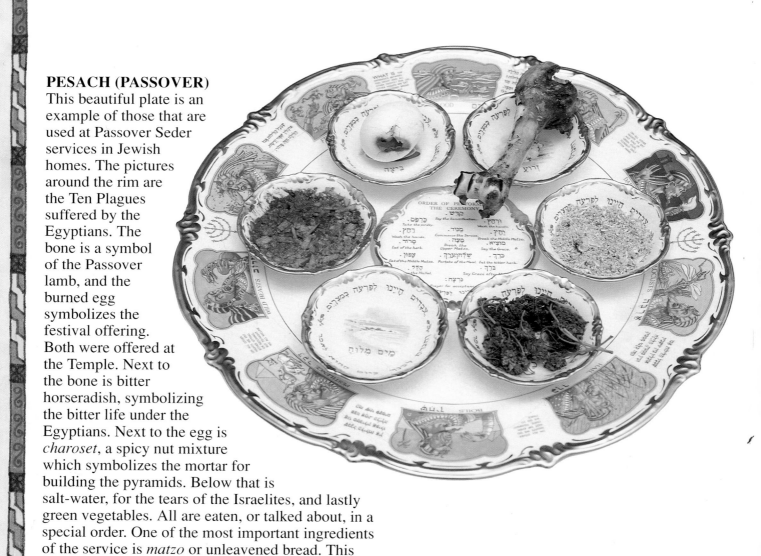

SHAVUOT

[It] is exactly seven weeks [after Pass]over. It commemorates [the giv]ing of the Torah. It is also [the fest]ival of the First Fruits, [which t]he Israeli children in the [photo]graph are celebrating. These [seven] weeks are known as the *Omer*. A 'countdown', looking forward to Shavuot, is made each night. Synagogues are decorated with flowers as a reminder that Mount Sinai was decorated by God in the same way for this miraculous occasion.

SUKKOT

At Sukkot all over the world some Jews build temporary huts. They eat in them, as the family in the photograph below is doing. The *sukkah,* or hut, is to remind them of the fragile dwellings in the wilderness, which were protected by God. It also reminds them of the huts that the farmers moved into at harvest time to be near their crops. The roof is made of cut branches and must be open to the sky. This family in Israel has lined the walls and hung up decorations.

THE SUKKOT HARVEST

There are seven types of food that were harvested at Sukkot time in Israel. Many Jews hang samples of each type of food from the ceiling of the sukkah to symbolize the harvest. These foods were: wheat, barley, grapes, olives, pomegranates, dates and figs.

THE LULAV AND ETROG

The *lulav*, or palm frond, is bound in a bundle, together with willow and myrtle branches. The *etrog*, a lemon-like citrus fruit, is used with this bundle in special blessings and ceremonies held during Sukkot. One tradition says that the palm frond represents the spine, the myrtle leaves are the eyes, the willow leaves the mouth, and the etrog the heart. This represents the worship of God with the whole body.

Lulav

Etrog

29

ARE·THERE ANY·OTHER ·JEWISH· FESTIVALS?

Unlike Rosh Hashanah, Yom Kippur and the Pilgrim Festivals, several festivals are not mentioned in the Torah, but they have existed for hundreds of years. *Purim* and *Chanukkah* began as permanent reminders of miraculous events in which God saved or helped the Jews against enormous odds. These festivals, and *Tu Bishvat*, the New Year for Trees, were recorded in the *Talmud* (the encyclopedia of Torah laws) before the end of the fifth century CE. *Simchat Torah*, the Festival of Rejoicing in the Torah, was introduced several hundred years later.

SIMCHAT TORAH

Reading and learning religious texts is one of the most important Jewish activities. It is customary to celebrate finishing the study of any Jewish book. The celebration for completing the annual cycle of reading the Torah is a joyous event. All the Torah scrolls are taken out of the Holy Ark. Members of the community are given the honor of dancing with the scrolls and circling the synagogue in processions, as in the photograph above.

 THE TORAH

The Torah consists of five books – the Five Books of Moses. Each of these books is divided into sections, known as *sidrot*. The first book is divided into 12, the second book into 11, the third into 10, the fourth into 10 and the fifth into 11, making 54 sidrot altogether. At least one section is read every Sabbath so that the whole cycle of readings is completed every year.

CHANUKKAH

Chanukkah celebrates the capture of the Temple from the Greeks and its re-dedication by the Maccabees, a Jewish resistance group. There was enough holy oil for the ever-burning *menorah* – the seven-branched candlestick – for only one day, but it lasted eight days, until more oil could be prepared. This is celebrated by lighting an extra light each night in an eight-branched menorah. Jews also eat foods cooked in oil.

Olive oil

Potato latkes

Doughnuts

TU BISHVAT

The New Year for Trees has been an important date since Talmudic times. It is often marked by planting new trees, especially those varieties mentioned in the *Tanakh* – the Jewish bible. The photograph on the right shows some female Israeli soldiers fulfilling their army service by working on national agricultural projects. As the date is 15 *Shevat*, Jews have the custom of eating fifteen different types of fruit to mark the day.

PURIM

Megillat Esther, the story of Purim, is read aloud from a parchment scroll, with much noise being made to drown out the name of Haman, the villain. As you can see in the photograph, people of all ages dress up and enjoy Purim feasts. Friends exchange gifts of food and give to the poor. Traditional foods include Purim loaves and *Hamantaschen,* or Haman's ears. These are triangular-shaped pastries, filled with jam or sweetened poppyseed paste.

Wine

Hamantaschen

WHAT·ARE THE·JEWS' ·HOLY· BOOKS?·

The holiest Jewish book is the Torah scroll, a parchment scroll on which the Five Books of Moses are handwritten. The Torah is the first part of the *Tanakh*. The second part is the *Nevi'im* – the books of the Prophets. The third part is the *Ketuvim* – all the other books of the Jewish bible, which include Psalms, Proverbs and the five *Megillot* (special stories or poems), each of which is associated with a festival. Prayerbooks and the books of the *Talmud* (dictated at Sinai, but not written down for centuries) are other Jewish holy books.

TORAH

The Torah scroll is wound on two wooden rollers. It is either encased in a richly embroidered cover and decorated with silver bells and crowns, or (as in the photograph on the left) mounted in a magnificent wooden case. The case on the left is highly decorated, both inside and out, and is traditional. The case stands upright on the reading desk for the Torah to be read.

 ### THE HEBREW ALPHABET

Hebrew is the language of the *Tenakh* and is a holy language. Each letter also represents a number. The Hebrew which is spoken in Israel today is similar to the Hebrew of the Torah. The *Talmud* is written in Aramaic. This was the everyday language of the Jews of Palestine and Babylon at the time it was written. Aramaic is written in Hebrew characters, which you can see below.

← **read from right to left**

Zayin	Vav	Hay	Dalet	Gimmel	Vet	Bet	Alef
Mem	Lammed	Final Chaf	Chaf	Kaf	Yud	Tet	Chet
Final Chaf	Fay	Pay	Ayin	Samech	Final Nun	Nun	Final mem
Tav	Tav	Sin	Shin	Raish	Kuf	Kaf	Tsadi

← **Vowels**

Chataf Segol	Chataf Patach	Chataf Kamats	Shuruk	Kubuts	Chirik	Holem	Sh'va	Segol	Tsayreh	Patach	Kamats

TELLING THE STORY

מַגִּיד

The head of the seder raises the Seder plate and shows the matzot.

This matzah is to remind us of the unleavened bread which our fathers ate as slaves in Egypt, many years ago. Whoever is hungry is invited to come eat with us. Whoever needs a Passover seder is welcome to join our seder.
This year we celebrate the Passover seder here. Next year we hope to celebrate in the Land of Israel.
This year we are like slaves. Next year we hope to be truly free.

הָא לַחְמָא עַנְיָא

דִּי אֲכָלוּ אַבְהָתָנָא בְּאַרְעָא דְמִצְרָיִם כָּל־דִּכְפִין יֵיתֵי וְיֵכָל כָּל־דִּצְרִיךְ יֵיתֵי וְיִפְסַח הָשַׁתָּא הָכָא לְשָׁנָה הַבָּאָה בְּאַרְעָא דְיִשְׂרָאֵל הָשַׁתָּא עַבְדֵי לְשָׁנָה הַבָּאָה בְּנֵי חוֹרִין

WASHING HANDS

וּרְחַץ

Wash hands without saying the blessing.

KARPAS

כַּרְפַּס

Dip a vegetable (boiled potato, parsley or celery) into salt water and say the blessing.

Blessed are You, Adonay, our God, King of the universe, who creates the produce of the earth.

בָּרוּךְ אַתָּה יי אֱלֹהֵינוּ מֶלֶךְ הָעוֹלָם בּוֹרֵא פְּרִי הָאֲדָמָה

DIVIDING THE MATZAH

יַחַץ

The three matzot are in place on the table. The head of the seder breaks the middle matzah and hides the larger piece, which somebody must find for the Afikoman after the meal.

THE HAGGADAH

The *Haggadah* contains the prayers, service and songs for the Passover Seder. It is one of the earliest Jewish books and there are still some copies in existence today that are more than 500 years old. Although every Haggadah contains the same basic contents, many have extra stories and songs and contain extra Jewish history. In many families, each member has his or her own Haggadah. Each person adds something to the service from this book. The modern Haggadah in the photograph above is designed for children, with attractive and colorful pictures, many featuring clay models.

THE SCRIBE

Torah scrolls and the scroll inside the mezuzah must be handwritten with a quill pen, on specially prepared parchment, with ink made to an ancient recipe. Writing a Torah scroll takes about a year. There are strict rules to follow as to how every word is written and spaced. The scribe is highly skilled and knows all the religious requirements of his art. In the photograph on the left, a scribe is writing a mezuzah scroll, with the words of the Shema prayer. Look at all his tools. Can you see in which direction the writing goes?

· W H O · ARE · THE · JEWISH LEADERS ?

From earliest times, Jewish leaders are believed by Jews to be men and women chosen by God as prophets to lead and teach the people. The Twelve Tribes were headed by princes. Later, when the Israelites were settled in Israel, they also had judges, kings and rabbis as leaders. Since the destruction of the Second Temple and the collapse of Israel as a country (until it was reinstated in 1948), rabbis have been the religious leaders. In Orthodox Judaism only male rabbis are allowed, but there are now a number of Reformed women rabbis.

SAUL AND DAVID

Saul was the first king of Israel. He used to have fits of depression and was often comforted by the harp music of a young man called David (his son Jonathan's best friend) as you can see in the painting. Later, Saul learned that David would succeed him as king, and tried to kill David, but Jonathan saved him. King David is famous for composing many psalms and making Jerusalem his capital.

 PROPHETS

There were many prophets who were leaders, including Moses, Aaron, Miriam and Joshua. They believed totally in God's justice, and constantly tried to persuade the Jewish people to behave decently among themselves and with other people. Famous prophets include: Samuel, Elijah, Jeremiah, Hosea, Jonah and Deborah, one of the few female leaders in the Tenakh.

MAIMONIDES

Maimonides, shown on the right, was also known as Rabbi Moses ben Maimon, or Rambam. He was born in the 12th century CE. He was one of the greatest medieval rabbis. His books are still studied today. Born in Spain, Maimonides later moved to Egypt to escape religious persecution and took up medicine. He became court physician, as well as a community leader, and continued to study Jewish law and philosophy.

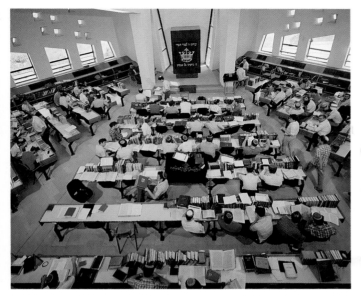

TRAINING TO BE A RABBI

Many young men go to a *yeshiva* – the college for rabbis – when they leave school. They study the holy books for up to 18 hours a day, as in the photograph on the left. Qualification for a rabbi is given only after years of study and written and oral examinations. Nowadays, many Orthodox rabbis and all Reformed rabbis study at a university for degrees. Modern rabbis are also trained in public speaking, counselling (advice) and a range of other skills needed for the modern world.

A Sephardi rabbi

THE RABBI AS LEADER

In the photograph above, the Chief Rabbi of the United Synagogues of Britain, Dr. Jonathan Sacks, presents a certificate of rabbinic ordination to a young graduate, Rabbi Broder. Rabbi Dr. Sacks is the leader of the largest group of Jews in Britain. In Israel, there are two chief rabbis, one for the *Ashkenazi* community (Western and European Jews), and one for the *Sephardi* community (Spanish, Portuguese and Oriental Jews). There are chief rabbis in other countries, such as France and Italy, but not in the USA. Many Reformed communities choose a rabbi to be leader or spokesperson for a number of years.

WHICH·ARE THE·JEWS' ·HOLY· ·PLACES?·

The holiest place in Judaism was the Temple, which was built on Mount Moriah in Jerusalem. It was destroyed by the Greeks. The second Temple was built on the same site, but destroyed by the Romans. Another holy place in Jerusalem is the Mount of Olives, a holy Jewish burial site. Although the burial places of Moses, Aaron and Miriam are not known, the burial sites of other leaders are places for pilgrimage and prayer. These include David's tomb, the Cave of Machpelah and the tombs of many famous rabbis. The tombs of Rabbi Maimonides and Rabbi Akiva, for example, are in Tiberias.

THE WESTERN WALL

The only remaining part of both Temples is the Western Wall, sometimes known as the Wailing Wall, in Jerusalem. Jewish and non-Jewish people from all over the world visit at all hours of the day and night, on weekdays, Sabbath and Jewish holidays. Jews push little pieces of paper with prayers and requests in between the holy stones of the Wall. They come to pray alone or with a group, and to feel close to God. As you can see in the photograph above, the area directly in front of the Wall is arranged so that men and women pray separately, divided by a screen.

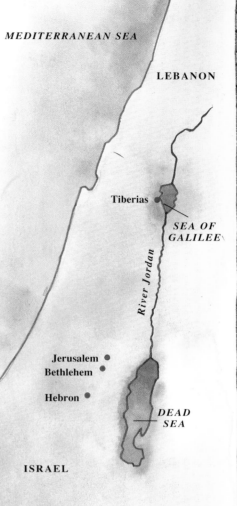

MOUNT OF OLIVES

The Mount of Olives, shown above, is the holiest Jewish burial site. This is because traditionally it is the route that the Messiah will take into Jerusalem when he comes to bring all the dead back to life. The people buried on the Mount of Olives will be the first to follow him into the Eternal Kingdom of

 CAVE OF MACHPELAH

The Cave of Machpelah, in Hebron, is the burial cave bought by Abraham. It is traditionally the burial place of Adam and Eve, Abraham and Sarah, Isaac and Rebekkah, and Jacob and Leah. Rachel, Jacob's favorite wife, was buried outside the original border of Israel, in Bethlehem.

Sites of Jewish holy places

JERUSALEM

Jerusalem is the holiest Jewish city on Earth, as it was the site of the two Temples for hundreds of years. However, it is also holy to Muslims and Christians. Therefore, it is important that people of all faiths can worship there freely. Jerusalem was set up as the capital of King David about 3,000 years ago, and has been captured by many rulers over the centuries. They wanted it to be only for members of their own faith. The Crusades (religious wars) began in 1096 CE because the Pope wanted to capture Jerusalem from the Muslims.

· W H A T · ARE · THE · JEWISH RITUAL OBJECTS ?

Judaism is a way of life and almost every Jewish activity has a special religious object associated with it. This may be a simple jug for hand-washing in the home, or the most ornate Torah scroll in the synagogue. Tradition encourages Jewish people to carry out religious duties willingly and with joy. Therefore, ritual objects are made of the best materials the owner can afford and decorated lovingly with embroidery and ornaments. If a Jew can afford only wood rather than silver, the wood should be beautifully carved and polished. With daily rituals like hand-washing, a more elaborate jug might be kept for Sabbath and the festivals.

THE HOLY ARK AND TORAH SCROLLS

Inside the richly decorated Holy Ark are the holy Torah scrolls. They are usually protected with an embroidered curtain, as well as wooden doors and wrought-iron gates. You can see the embroidered curtain in the photograph, pulled back to the left. Those scrolls at the back of the Ark are sometimes old and not fit for use, but they are still treasured. Those that are used have silver breastplates, pointers and bells or crowns, as well as embroidered velvet covers.

 SPICE BOXES

In the Havdalah ceremony at the end of Sabbath, a box of spices is passed around for each person to smell. This is to refresh the soul for the coming week. To make the ceremony even more special, the spice boxes are often beautifully decorated and designed as castles, windmills and towers. They are carved from wood or made of decorated silver, glass or china.

TORAH POINTERS

Pointers, used to mark the place while reading from the Torah, are often made of silver. The end is sometimes shaped like a fist with a finger pointing. Pointers are used because the Torah scroll must not be touched by hand.

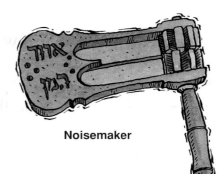

Noisemaker

Silver pointers

NOISEMAKERS

When reading the story of Purim, Jews are commanded to drown out the name of the villain, Haman, whenever it is read out loud (see page 31).

MARRIAGE CERTIFICATE

The *ketubah* – marriage certificate – not only sets out the details of the marriage, but also contains details of the money and goods the groom must give his bride if the marriage ends in divorce. Marriage certificates are often handwritten and beautifully decorated like the one above. They may be on display in the home.

Dreidls

SPINNING TOPS

The *dreidl*, or *sevivon*, is a spinning top for use on Chanukkah. It has four Hebrew letters, which stand for 'a Great Miracle Happened There'. Each letter is also an instruction to give or take counters in a game.

THE ETERNAL LIGHT

The *Ner Tamid,* or Eternal Light, is found hanging from the ceiling of the synagogue. As you can see in the photograph on the right, it is directly in front of the Holy Ark. The light, inside its ornate container, burns all the time in many synagogues. With electricity this is no longer a problem! The Ner Tamid is a symbol of the menorah in the Temple, in which the purest olive oil was burned. It is also a reminder that the Torah is the guiding light of the Jews.

·DO·JEWS· HAVE·A· TRADITION ·OF·MUSIC- MAKING?

There is a very strong tradition of Jewish music-making. This is recorded as far back as the time of the Exodus from Egypt. There were musical instruments made especially for use in the Temple. In many Orthodox synagogues, musical instruments are never used on Sabbath or on festival days, the only music being singing. However, many Reformed synagogues do use musical instruments in their services. Folk-songs are found in every Jewish community. They are used to comfort, to entertain and to pass on history and traditions.

MIRIAM AND THE WOMEN

After the Israelites' miraculous escape from the pursuing Egyptians at the Red Sea, Moses composed a hymn to God. This is recorded in the Torah, for all to sing. Miriam took the women off separately to dance and sing the hymn, playing on her timbrel, as the painting shows. At many Orthodox weddings, it is still customary for women and men to dance and sing separately.

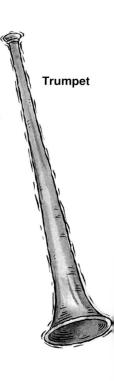

Trumpet

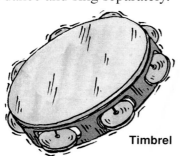

Timbrel

Cymbals

MUSIC IN THE TANAKH

In the *Tanakh*, many musical instruments are mentioned. Perhaps the most famous are: Miriam's timbrel – a type of tambourine; King David's lyre – a small harp; and the shofar – the ram's horn. The noise from the shofar brought down the walls of Jericho. When the Israelites were camped in the desert, silver trumpets were blown to call the tribes either to a meeting, or to march, or to war. Bugles are used in much the same way in modern armies. As well as harps and lyres, flutes, cymbals and trumpets were played in the Temple. Other instruments mentioned in the *Tanakh* are drums, bells and clappers or rattles.

WEDDING MUSIC

It is considered especially important to make the bride happy at her wedding. A Jewish wedding is not complete without its musicians. As well as special tunes for psalms and hymns, there are some hauntingly beautiful melodies composed especially for weddings. Today, the bride is often escorted to the wedding canopy with beautiful singing by a cantor or choir. At the celebratory meal, the couple are entertained with happy songs and instrumental tunes. A traditional group of musicians, known as *klezmer* musicians, used to provide the music in each town or village for special occasions.

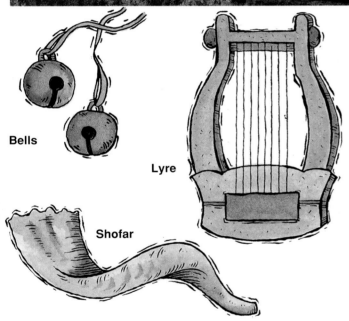

Bells

Lyre

Shofar

FOLK-DANCING

There are many Jewish folk-dances. Some date from biblical times and use songs and poems from the *Tanakh*. Others are from countries in which Jews lived for centuries, such as Russia and the Arab lands. Sometimes they use Jewish dances and words, but the tunes come from the host countries. For Jews in many lands folk-dancing is popular as a hobby, at weddings and for all festive occasions, as you can see in the photograph on the right.

All of the laws and traditions of Judaism have been passed down for generations through story-telling. At the Passover Seder service, the whole family is expected to sit around the table. They tell and re-tell the story of the slavery of the Jews in Egypt, the Ten Plagues and the eventual Exodus from Egypt, as if each member of the family had personally left Egypt. The Torah itself, the rest of the *Tanakh* and the *Talmud* teach their historical, social, ethical and legal lessons largely through story-telling. The greatest Jewish teachers have often been those who could put over their lessons in dramatic or witty stories.

JONAH AND THE BIG FISH

The book of Jonah the Prophet, from the *Tenakh*, teaches repentance and forgiveness. Jonah refuses God's command to instruct the people of Nineveh (a Middle-Eastern city) to be sorry for their evil ways. He tries to escape from God by taking a ship to Spain. The ship is struck by a storm. Jonah, realizing this is his punishment, insists on being thrown overboard. The storm stops and he is swallowed by an enormous fish (as shown in the painting). After praying to God, Jonah is thrown up on land and agrees to go to Nineveh. He persuades the people to repent and they are also forgiven by God.

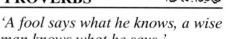

SAYINGS AND PROVERBS

Throughout the *Tanakh*, the *Talmud* and many of the other Jewish holy books, there are many wise and witty sayings and proverbs that are still used today.

Here are just a few examples:

'Do not judge a man until you have stood in his place.'

'A fool says what he knows, a wise man knows what he says.'

'In the country of the blind, the one-eyed man is king.'

'Do not do to others what you would not like them to do to you.'

'God gave man one mouth and two ears so that he could listen twice as much as he could speak.'

RABBI AKIVA

Rabbi Akiva (50–135 CE) was one of the greatest rabbis of his time. Many of his rulings are given in the *Talmud*. There are also dozens of stories that he told, and which were told about him, to comfort and strengthen his followers during the time of Roman oppression in which they lived.

His own life story is a great romance. Starting life as a poor shepherd boy, Akiva ben Joseph fell in love with his wealthy master's daughter, Rachel. Although her father cast them out without a penny, Rachel insisted, as a condition of their marriage, that Akiva become a Torah scholar. They were so poor that Rachel had to sell her hair so that they could eat. However, they both heroically carried on with their intentions.

Eventually, Akiva became a great scholar and Rachel's father, ashamed of his lack of faith in his daughter, begged their forgiveness. Rabbi Akiva died a martyr's death. He was burned alive by the Romans for teaching the Torah. However, to the wonder of his followers, he died with great dignity and even joy. He said that he finally understood and could carry out the command of the Shema prayer – to love God with all his heart and soul.

CHILDREN LISTENING TO A STORY
These Jewish children are learning about Jewish traditions through listening to stories. The stories may be from the Torah, or they may be new stories. These help them to understand what being Jewish means to them.

THE TORCH, THE COCKEREL AND THE DONKEY

Once, Rabbi Akiva went on a journey, riding on a donkey. He carried with him a rooster to wake him in the morning and a torch of burning pitch to light his way in the dark. He finally came to a small village, but no one was willing to give him a bed for the night. Instead of being angry, he just shrugged his shoulders and said, 'Whatever is God's will is for the best', and he went out of the village to sleep in a field. During the night, a lion killed and carried off the donkey, a fox feasted on the rooster, and a strong wind blew out the torch. He accepted each disaster as God's will.

Next morning, he awoke to find that the village had been attacked by armed robbers in the night. They had killed all the people and stolen their goods.

'I see now that all is in God's hand', he said to himself. 'Had the people been more hospitable, I would have stayed with them. Had my torch stayed alight, my donkey brayed or my rooster crowed, the robbers would have found me, even in the field, and killed me too.'

·GLOSSARY·

BAR MITZVAH A Jewish boy who reaches the age of 13 is a Bar Mitzvah. This means he is considered a man in Jewish law. He must keep all the laws that apply to Jewish men.

BAT MITZVAH A Jewish girl who reaches the age of 12 is a Bat Mitzvah. This means that she is considered a woman in Jewish law. She must keep all the laws that apply to Jewish women.

CHANUKKAH The Feast of the Re-dedication of the Temple. It lasts for eight days. It begins on 25 *Kislev* and commemorates the events of 140–138 BCE.

CIRCUMCISION The act of cutting off the loose skin at the tip of the penis known as the foreskin. It is a sign of the covenant Abraham made with God.

COVENANT In the *Tenakh*, a covenant is a solemn agreement between God and human beings. Usually, God gives a sign to show that he will keep his promise and the human beings do something important to show that they will keep their promise.

HASIDIC JEWS Jews who follow the branch of Judaism known as Hasidism. Each Hasidic group was founded by a leader, known as a Rebbe.

ISRAELITES The name given to the people who were descendants of Israel, as Jacob was later known. The name 'Jews' was adopted much later. The Israelites were permanently divided into twelve tribes for every activity. Each tribe consisted of the direct male descendants of one of Jacob's sons, plus their wives, families and servants. Each tribe had its own place to live and duties to carry out.

KOSHER Kosher food is food that the Torah lists as being suitable for Jews to eat. It includes any fruit and vegetables, cereals and other foods which grow in the ground or on trees and bushes. Only fish with fins and scales, such as cod, animals which eat grass and vegetables (and chew the cud) and have split hooves, such as cows, and a list of named birds, such as chickens, are permitted. Animals and birds must be killed in a special way called 'Shechitah' and all blood must be drained away before the flesh can be eaten.

MATZO Unleavened bread, made only of flour and water, but no yeast. It is the bread that slaves used to eat in Egypt. It is flat and crispy.

MIKVEH A pool of 'living' water, from either rain, a river or the sea. Objects or people are completely dipped in mikveh water as a sign of religious purity.

PASSOVER The festival of freedom from slavery. In Israel it lasts for seven days and eight days outside Israel, beginning on 15 *Nisan*. It commemorates the Exodus of the Children of Israel from slavery in Egypt.

PURIM The Feast of Lots, celebrated each year on 14 *Adar*. Haman, the Persian Prime Minister, cast lots to see which was the best day for killing all the Jews in the Empire of King Xerxes II. The Jewish Queen, Esther, and Mordechai her uncle, exposed Haman. The Festival of Purim was established to mark the miraculous survival of the Jews.

ROSH HASHANAH The New Year, celebrated each year on 1 and 2 *Tishrei*. The Jewish New Year is a time for thinking about your actions of the past year, and making plans to improve yourself for the coming year.

SABBATH The seventh day of Creation. On this day, God rested from doing any further work. In the fourth of the Ten Commandments, Jews are told to remember this day every week, to rest and keep it holy.

SHAVUOT The Festival of the First Fruits. It is also the Festival of the Giving of the Torah.

SUKKOT The Harvest Festival, celebrated for seven days. The eighth day is known as *Shemini Atzeret*.

TABERNACLE The Tabernacle was the magnificent tent of meeting, prayer and sacrifice which was made by the Israelites in the Wilderness, at God's command. It was the original home of the two stone tablets engraved with the Ten Commandments, located inside their precious golden box, the Ark. The Tabernacle was portable and was taken with the Israelites wherever they went. The Ark was always taken with the Israelites when they fought wars, to give them courage and strength.

TALLIT A prayer shawl with fringes at each of the four corners. Orthodox men wrap themselves in a prayer shawl for many prayer services. Progressive Jews permit both men and women to wear the tallit.

TALMUD A collection of 63 books containing interpretations of the Bible and rabbinical commentaries.

TEFILLIN Tefillin are two small square boxes that contain the Shema prayer and other paragraphs from the Torah, attached to the head and arm by leather straps.

TEMPLE The first Temple was built by King Solomon, son of King David, to be the holiest place for prayers and sacrifices. It was where the two stone tablets engraved with the Ten Commandments inside the Holy Ark were housed. It was destroyed by the Greeks. A replacement was built which was later destroyed by the Romans. Orthodox Jews pray every day for the Temple to be rebuilt.

TORAH The first written part of the Jewish bible. It consists of the Five Books of Moses.

YARMULKE (or kippah) A small round cap that Jewish boys and men wear on top of their heads. Some only wear a yarmulke when praying, some wear it all day .

YOM KIPPUR The Day of Atonement, the most solemn festival. It is also a 25-hour fast.

· I N D E X ·